LEVEL 4

PIANO
Adventures®

Arranged by Nancy and Randall Faber

A BASIC PIANO METHOD

Production: Frank and Gail Hackinson
Production Coordinator: Philip Groeber
Editors: Edwin McLean and Joanne Smith
Cover and Illustrations: Terpstra Design, San Francisco
Engraving: Tempo Music Press, Inc.
Printer: Vicks

FABER
PIANO ADVENTURES®
3042 Creek Drive
Ann Arbor, Michigan 48108

ISBN 978-1-61677-315-1

A Note to Teacher and Parents

For decades, popular repertoire has captured the hearts of people worldwide. Perhaps it is the memorable melodies, engaging lyrics, and catchy rhythms that create its magic and universal appeal. Some of America's finest music makers have left us a legacy that will be treasured for all time—John Kander's *New York, New York;* John Williams' Theme from *Jurassic Park;* and Jerry Walker's *Mr. Bojangles.*

Piano Adventures® Popular Repertoire (Level 4) offers a unique teaching experience for teacher and student alike. Outstanding popular repertoire has been skillfully arranged and correlated with the concepts in the *Piano Adventures® Lesson Book* (Level 4). A notable feature of *Piano Adventures® Popular Repertoire* is the music activity page that follows each popular selection. At Level 4, these pages imaginatively engage the student in harmony, ear training, rhythm, sightreading, and improvisation. A music dictionary at the end of the book provides a quick and easy reference for basic musical terms.

So have fun! America's finest popular repertoire has now been pedagogically presented with what many are calling the finest method ever—*Piano Adventures®*!

CONTENTS

Changing Time Signature

When changing from one time signature to another, the pulse (beat) remains the same. (See *measures 6* and *7*.)

Theme from
"Jurassic Park"

Key of _____ Major

Composed by
John Williams

FF1

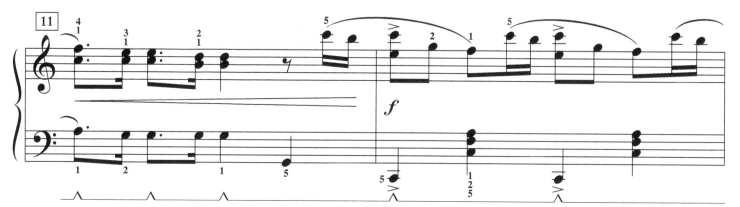

Find two measures where the L.H. plays the melody.

Jurassic Chords

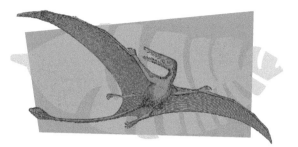

The **I**, **IV**, and **V** (or **V7**) chords are called the *primary* chords because they are the most common chords in music.

They are built on *scale degrees* 1, 4, and 5.

• Find and play the primary chords in the **Key of C Major** shown below.

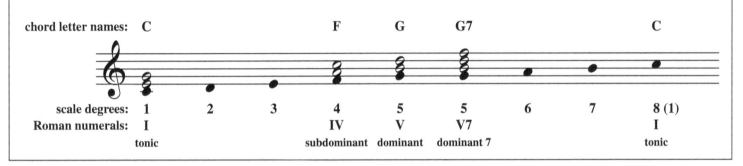

chord letter names:	C			F	G	G7			C
scale degrees:	1	2	3	4	5	5	6	7	8 (1)
Roman numerals:	I			IV	V	V7			I
	tonic			subdominant	dominant	dominant 7			tonic

Analyze the harmony for each example given.

• Write **C**, **F**, **G**, or **G7** in the boxes *above* the grand staff.

• Write **I**, **IV**, **V**, or **V7** on the line *below* the grand staff.
  Note: Several chords are in an inversion.

Theme from
"Jurassic Park"

Composed by
John Williams

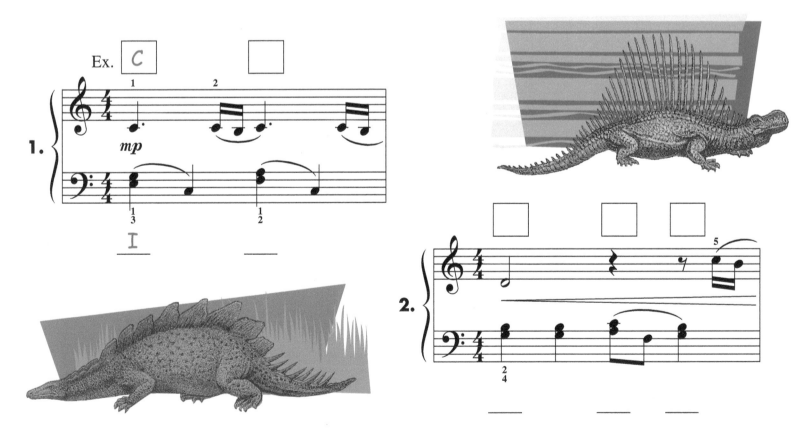

FF13

3.

4.

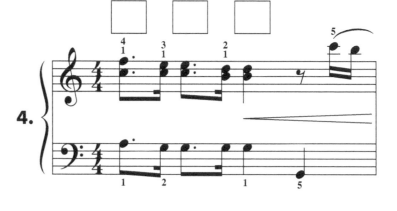

5.

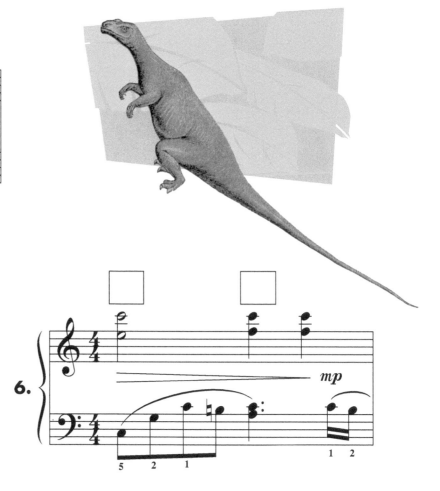

6.

Swing Review:

If the *tempo mark* includes the word "swing," play the 8th notes with a *long–short* swing rhythm.

Mr. Bojangles

Key of _____ Major

Words and Music by
Jerry Jeff Walker

Moderate waltz, in swing (♩♩ = ♩ ♪)

knew a man Bo-jan - gles and he danced___ for you

in worn - out shoes. With

sil - ver hair, a rag - ged shirt, and bag - gy pants,

the old soft shoe.

FF13

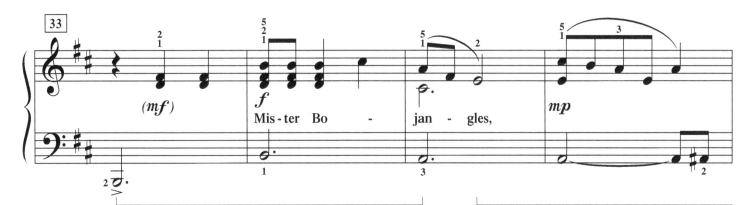

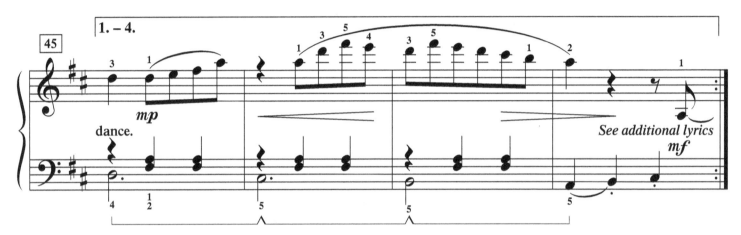

2. I met him in a cell in New Orleans, I was down and out.
   He looked at me to be the eyes of age as he spoke right out.
   He talked of life, talked of life;
   He laughed, slapped his leg a step. *To Chorus*

3. He said his name, Bojangles, then danced a lick across the cell.
   He grabbed his pants, a better stance, oh, he jumped up high; he clicked his heels.
   He let go a laugh, let go a laugh,
   Shook back his clothes all around. *To Chorus*

4. He danced for those at minstrel shows and county fairs throughout the South.
   He spoke with tears of fifteen years how his dog and he traveled about.
   His dog up and died; he up and died;
   After twenty years he still grieved. *To Chorus*

5. He said, "I dance now at ev'ry chance in honky-tonks for drinks and tips.
   But most of the time I spend behind these county bars." He said, "I drinks a bit."
   He shook his head and as he shook his head,
   I heard someone ask, please: *To Chorus*

Name the **major** chord used in *measure 1*.
What inversion does the R.H. play?

Bojangles' Bass

Popular music often has descending scale tones in the bass part—the **bass line**. This page explores the descending bass line of *Mr. Bojangles.*

When the bass note is *different* than the **root** of the chord (chord letter name), this symbol is used:

D/C♯ means $\dfrac{\text{D major chord}}{\text{C♯ in the bass}}$

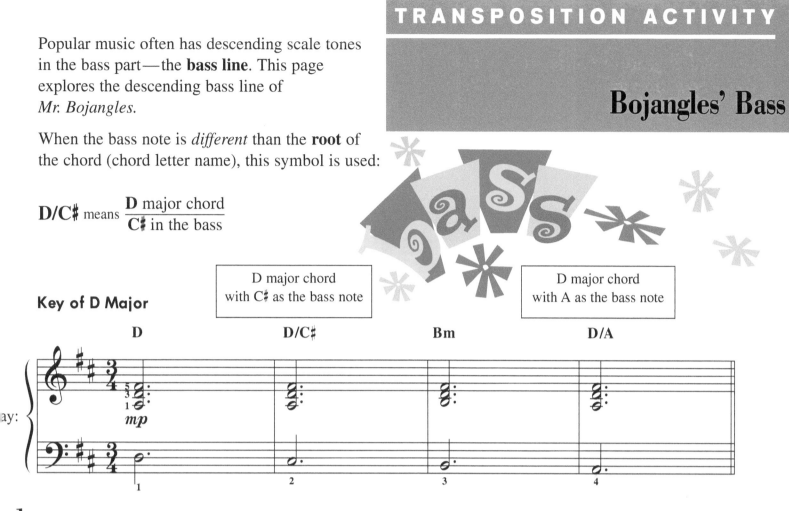

D major chord with C♯ as the bass note

D major chord with A as the bass note

Key of D Major

1. Complete the **chord symbols** by filling in the shaded boxes. Then play.

Key of ____ Major

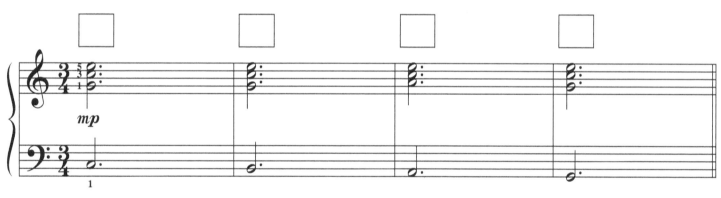

Key of ____ Major

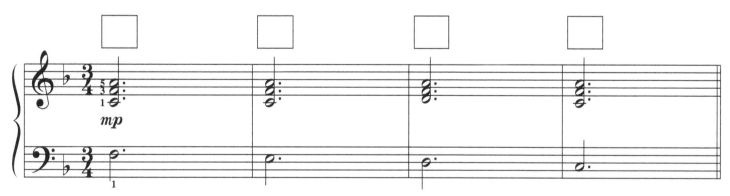

2. Transpose the example above to the Key of G Major. (The R.H. begins with a *2nd inversion* chord.)

G   **G/F♯**   **Em**   **G/D**

If You Believe

Key of _____ Major

Composed by
Jim Brickman

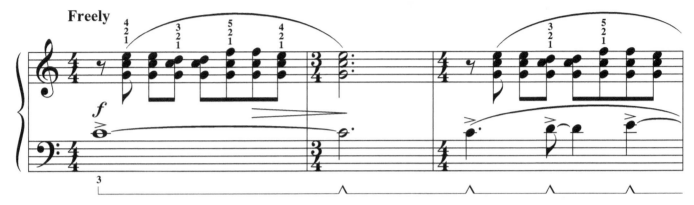

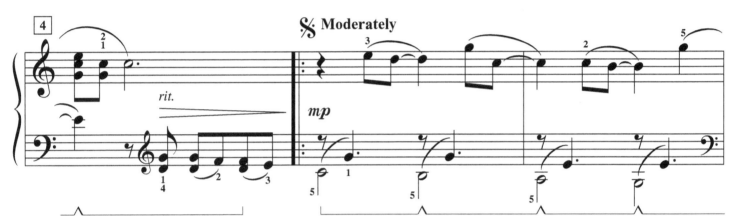

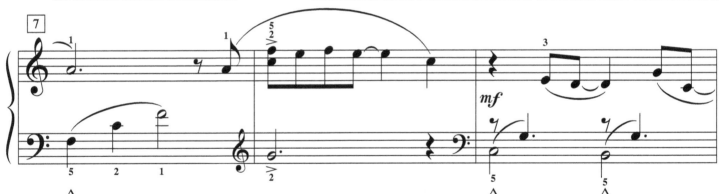

FF13

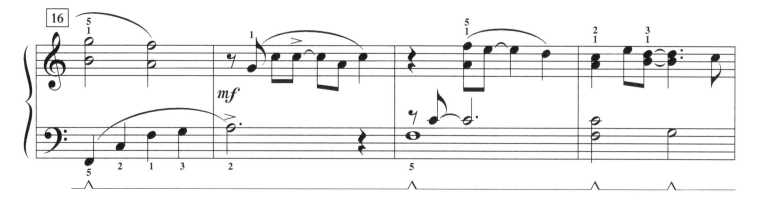

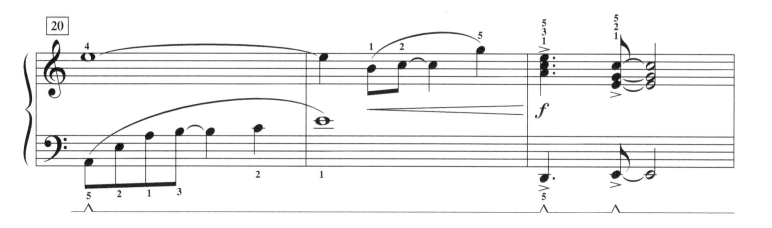

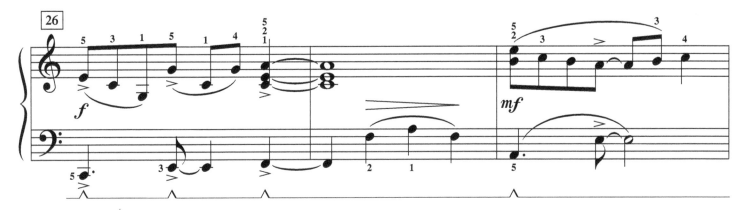

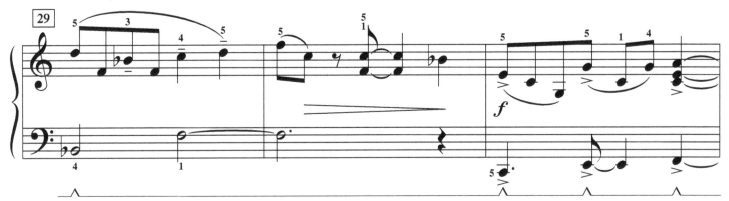

14

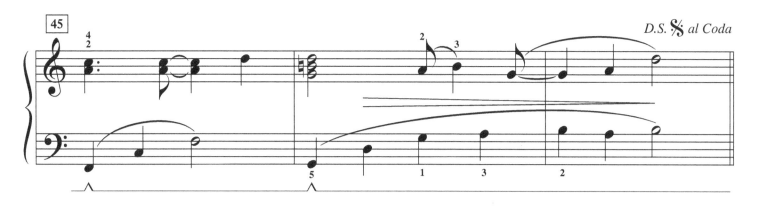

D.S. 𝄋 al Coda

Coda

Freely

DISCOVERY

Can you find a changing **time signature**?

Theory Class

If You Believe

Composed by
Jim Brickman

Study the music for *If You Believe* to complete the following information.

1. Name the key for *If You Believe:* _____ major or minor *(circle)*

Write the letter names for the primary chords (**I, IV, V**):

_____ major, _____ major, _____ major

2a. Write the counts **1 + 2 + 3 + 4 +** for this measure. (**+** = and)

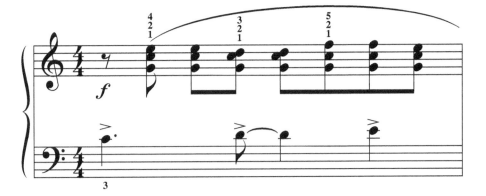

b. Play each hand separately, counting aloud. Then play hands together, counting aloud.

3. Find a two-measure **descending bass line** (C–B–A–G) on the first page of *If You Believe.*

measures _____ and _____

4. Write the **chord names** in the boxes. Choose from these chords: **C, Dm, Em, F, G, Am**
Indicate the bass note if it is *not* the root of the chord. Ex. **C/E** (See p. 11 for review.)
(Answers are upside down at bottom of the page.)

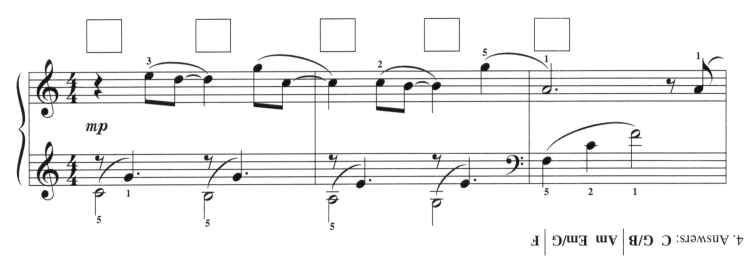

4. Answers: C | G/B | Am Em/G | F

FF13

5. Syncopation is a change from the normal pattern of accent. Instead of accenting the strong beats of the measure, the accent occurs *between* the beats—on the *offbeats*.

- Write the counts **1 + 2 + 3 + 4 +** for the example below.

- Then circle the *offbeat* where the syncopation occurs.

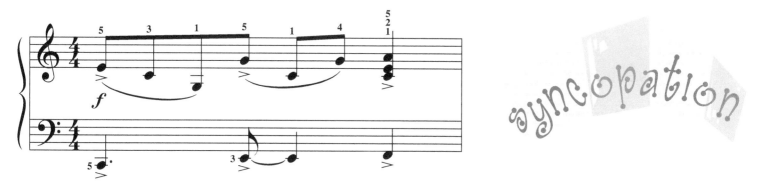

6. Name the **major chord** outlined in the measure below. Circle the note that is *not* a chord tone.

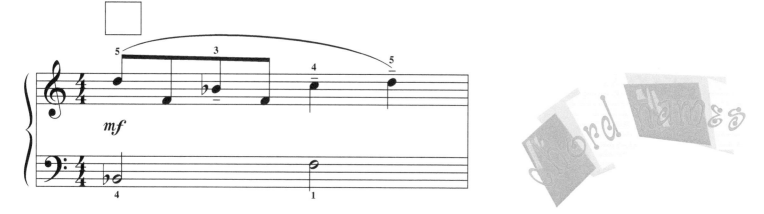

7. Find a 13-note **descending bass line** in *If You Believe (measures 38–44)*.
Write the descending bass line on the staves below. Use half notes.

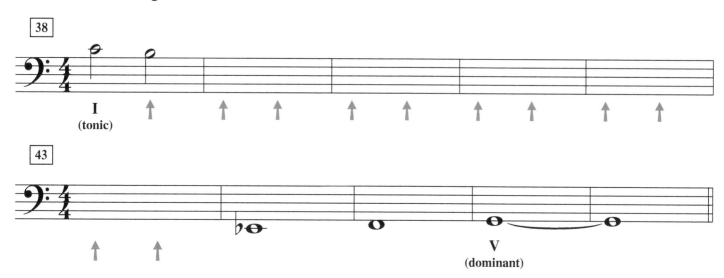

8. In the **coda** *(measure 48),* find an **ascending bass line** that steps up to the *dominant* (scale degree 5).

Circle these four bass notes in your music. Then name them in the blanks below.

_____ , _____ , _____ , _____

The Greatest Love of All

Key of _____ Major

Words by
Linda Creed

Music by
Michael Masser

FF13

be. Ev-'ry-bod-y's search-ing for a he-ro; peo-ple need some-one to look___ up to.

Nev-er found an-y-one who ful-filled that need; a lone-ly

place to be, so I learned to de-pend on

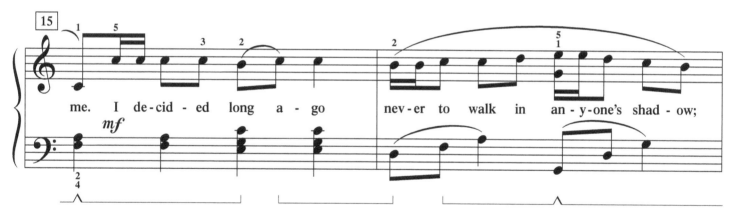

me. I de-cid-ed long a-go nev-er to walk in an-y-one's shad-ow;

if I fail, if I suc-ceed, at least I lived as I be-lieve.___ No

mat-ter what they take from me, they can't take a-way my dig-ni-ty. Be-cause the

great - est love of all___ is hap-pen-ing to me.

I find the great - est love of all___ in-side of

me. The great-est love of all_____ is eas-y to a-

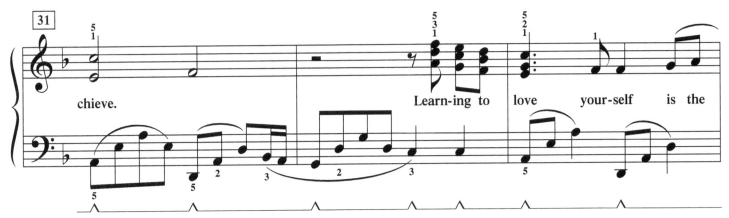

chieve. Learn-ing to love your-self is the

great - est love of all. And if by chance that

spe - cial place that you've been dream-ing of

leads you to a lone - ly place, find your strength in

love.

DISCOVERY

Write the **chord symbols** above the harmony changes for *measures 37–42.*

Notice that this pattern occurs three times: **Em Am | Dm G |**

It's easy to achieve...

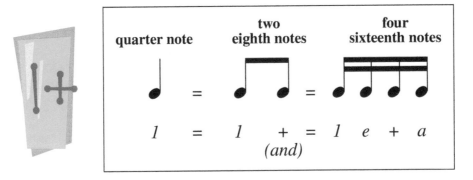

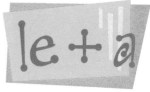

- Draw an arrow over each *main* beat: **1 2 3 4**

- Next, subdivide each beat by writing **1 e + a   2 e + a   3 e + a   4 e + a**.

- Then, play the rhythms using a *blocked* chord for each note.

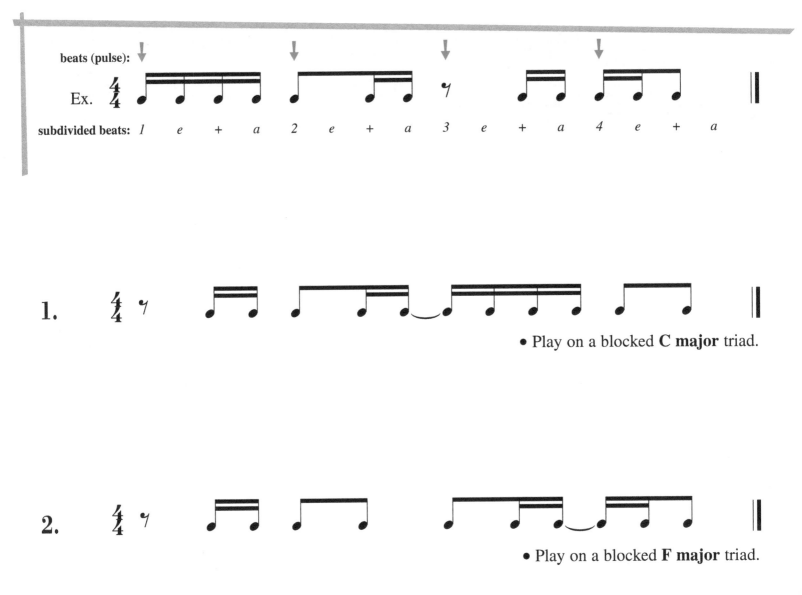

- Play on a blocked **C major** triad.

- Play on a blocked **F major** triad.

FF131

3.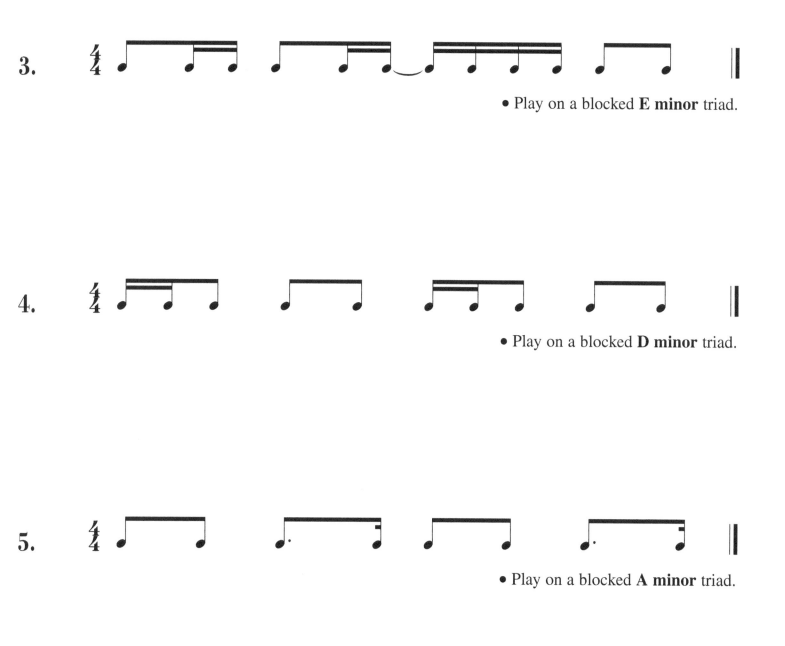

• Play on a blocked **E minor** triad.

4.

• Play on a blocked **D minor** triad.

5.

• Play on a blocked **A minor** triad.

6. Now write two measures of your own rhythm in $\frac{4}{4}$ time, using **16th notes**.

Choose from these 16th-note patterns:

• Play your rhythm on a major or minor triad *of your choice*.

Extra Credit: Add one or more *ties* to your rhythm. Then play, counting aloud.

Theme from
New York, New York

Key of _____ Major

Words by
Fred Ebb

Music by
John Kander

Moderately, with swing

FF13

and step a - round the heart___ of it, New York, New York.

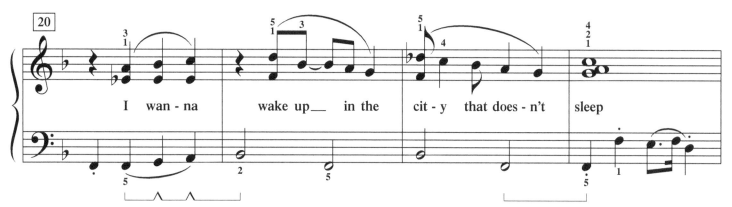

I wan - na wake up___ in the cit - y that does - n't sleep

to find I'm king of the hill,___ top of the heap.

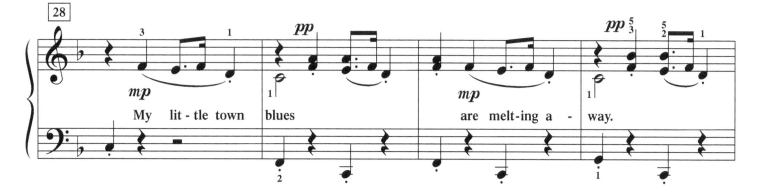

My lit - tle town blues are melt - ing a - way.

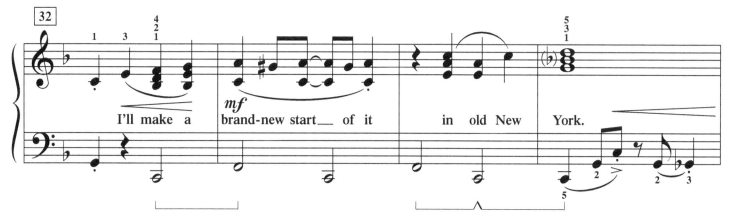

I'll make a brand-new start___ of it in old New York.

F1315

25

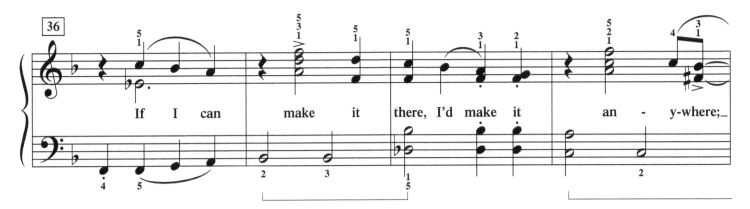

If I can make it there, I'd make it an - y-where;

_ it's up to you, New York, New York. *mp*

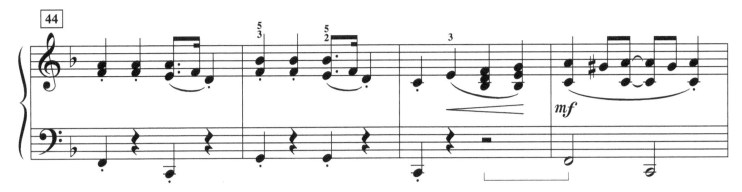

mf

New York, New York. I wan - na wake up_ in the

cit - y that does - n't sleep to find I'm king of the hill,_ *f*

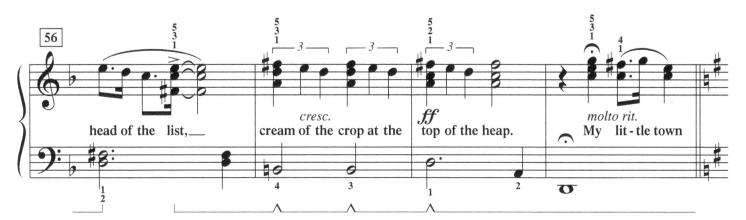

head of the list,___ cream of the crop at the top of the heap. My lit-tle town

cresc. *ff* *molto rit.*

Slowly, broadly

blues are melt-ing a - way; I'll make a

f *mf*

brand-new start___ of it in old New York. If I can

f

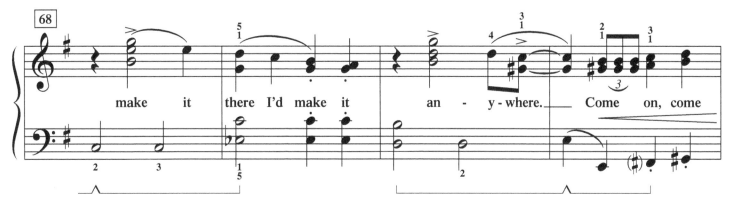

make it there I'd make it an - y - where.___ Come on, come

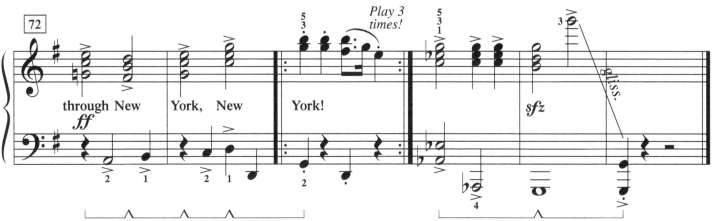

through New York, New York! *Play 3 times!*

ff *sfz* *gliss.*

1315

27

Balance Within the Hand

Sometimes one hand will play both *melody* and *harmony* notes.

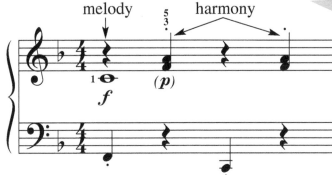

For melody notes:
Drop with arm weight to the bottom of the key for a full, rich tone.

For harmony notes:
Play from the surface of the key, using a *light* touch.

In this etude, each R.H. whole note must "sing" above the R.H. harmony.

The shaded boxes will remind you which finger is "king of the hill."

"King of the Hill" Etude

based on music by John Kander

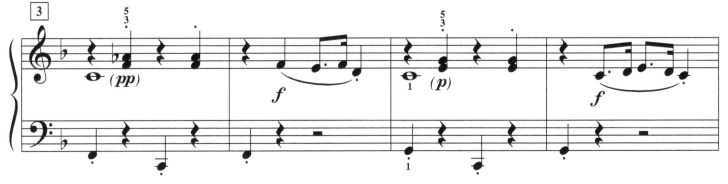

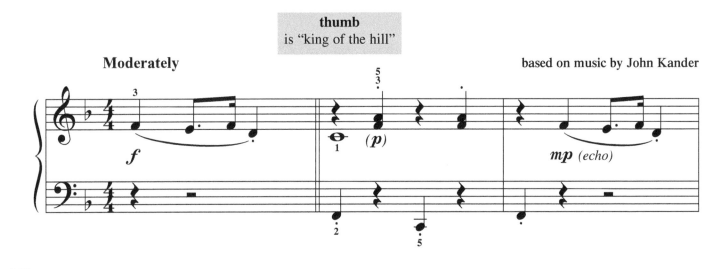

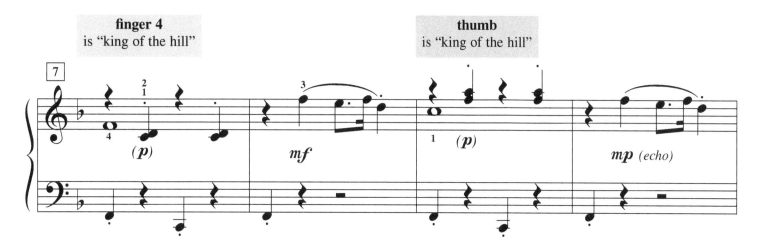

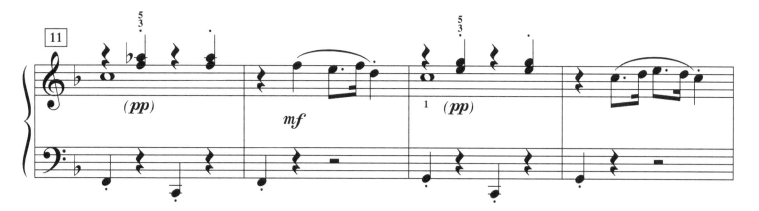

The Way It Is

Key of _____ Major

Words and Music by
Bruce Hornsby

Moderate Rock beat

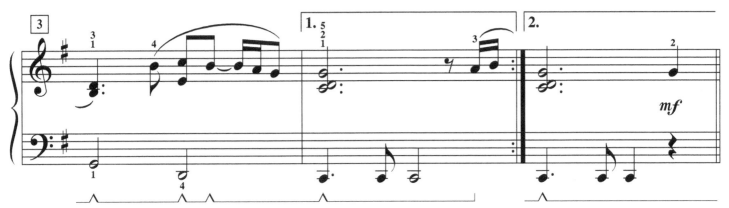

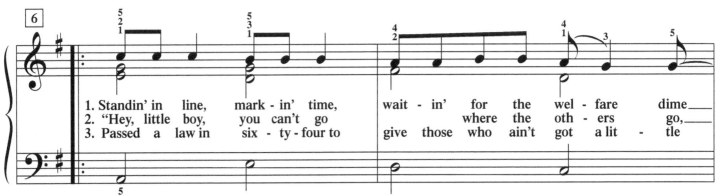

1. Standin' in line, mark - in' time, wait - in' for the wel - fare dime ____ 'cause they can't buy a job.
2. "Hey, little boy, you can't go where the oth - ers go, 'cause you don't look like they do." The
3. Passed a law in six - ty - four to give those who ain't got a lit - tle more, but it on - ly goes so far.

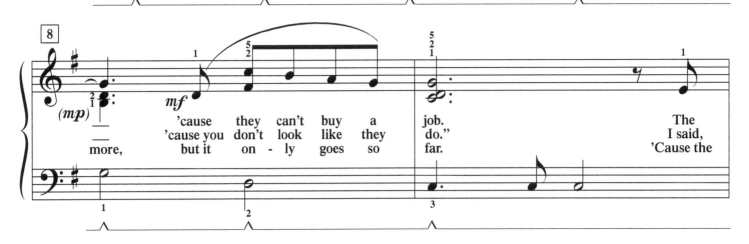

'cause they can't buy a job.
'cause you don't look like they do."
more, but it on - ly goes so far.

The
I said,
'Cause the

FF13

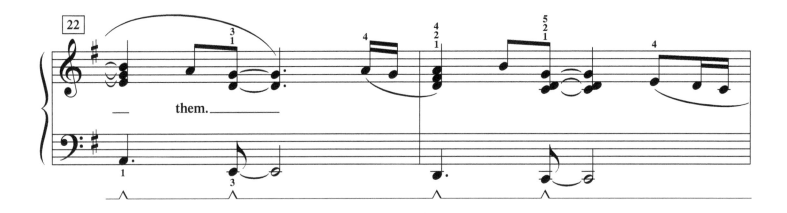

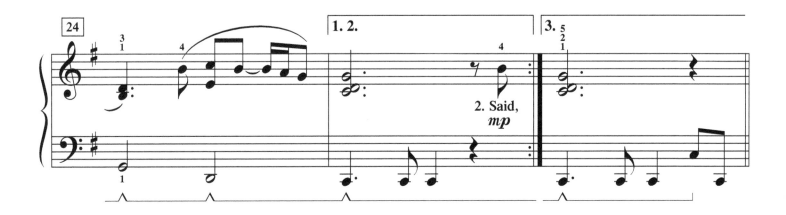

Ah, but don't you be - lieve

them.

2. Said,

repeat and fade

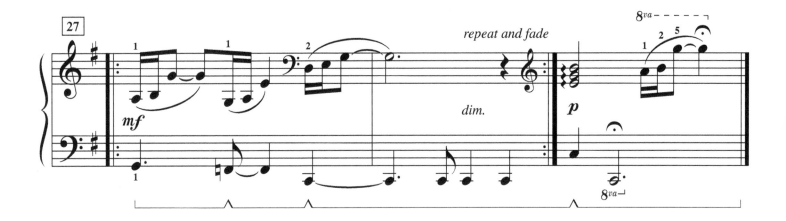

DISCOVERY

The **pick-up** notes in this piece begin on which part of the beat? *(circle)*

1 + 2 + 3 + 4 +

The Way It Should Be

Your teacher will play **example a** or **b**.

- *Listen* carefully and circle the example you hear.

The Way It Is

Words and Music by
Bruce Hornsby

Extra Credit: Play each example above.

Ashokan Farewell

Key of _____ Major

By
Jay Ungar

Rather slowly, plaintively

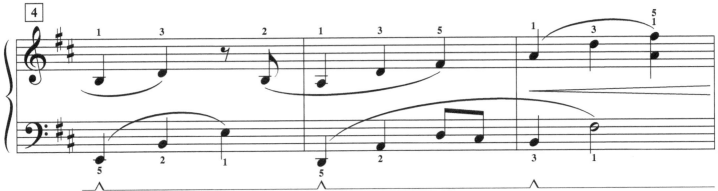

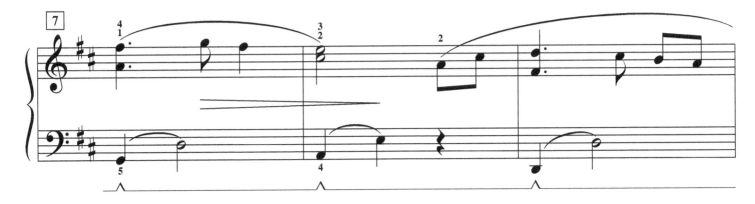

FF13

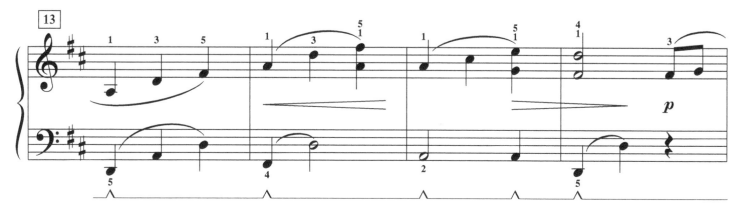

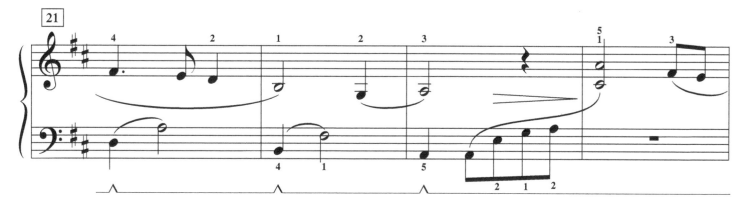

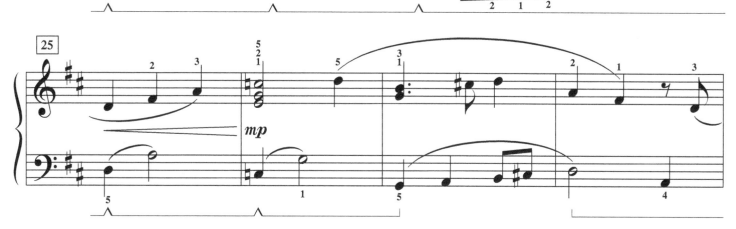

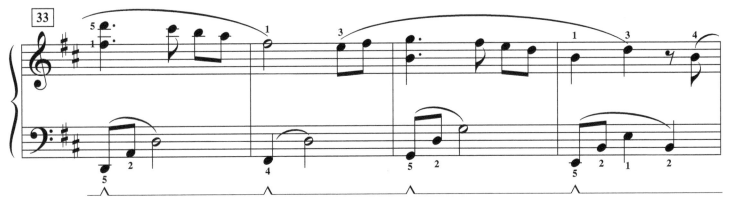

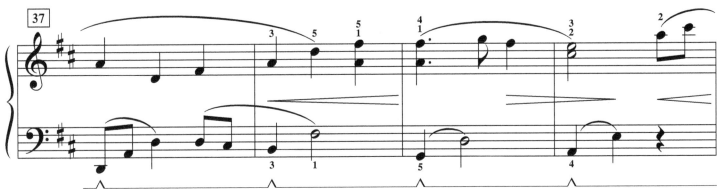

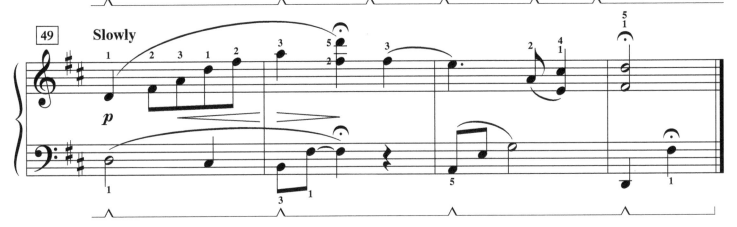

DISCOVERY

In which measure does the opening theme return one octave higher? *measure* ____

Ashokan Variations

- Scan each example for **rhythm**, **shape of the melody**, and **dynamics**.

- Sightread the examples below. Then transpose to the key suggested.

based on music by Jay Ungar

- Transpose to the **Key of C Major**.

Notice R.H. finger 2 begins on *scale degree 5*.

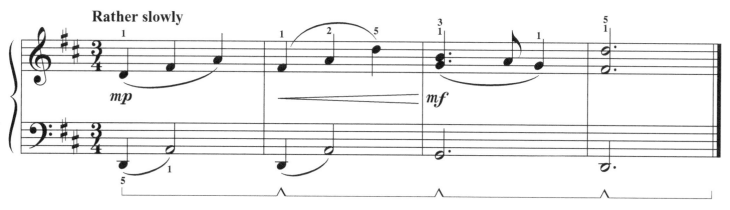

- Transpose to the **Key of G Major**.

Notice the melody begins with a *root position,* then *1st inversion* chord.

- Transpose to the **Key of C Major**.

Notice L.H. plays root position **I**, **IV**, and **V** broken triads.

1315

Key Signature of A Major

The 3 sharps for A Major:

F♯   C♯   G♯

G♯ is the *leading tone*.

I Will Remember You

Key of _____ Major

Words and Music by
Sarah McLachlan, Seamus Egan,
and David Merenda

Moderately slow

mp

I will re-mem-ber you. ___ Will you re-mem-ber me?

Don't let your life ___ pass ___ you by,

pp

weep not for ___ the mem - o - ries. ___

mf

1. I'm so tired, ___ I can't sleep, ___
2. *See additional lyrics*

FF1

315

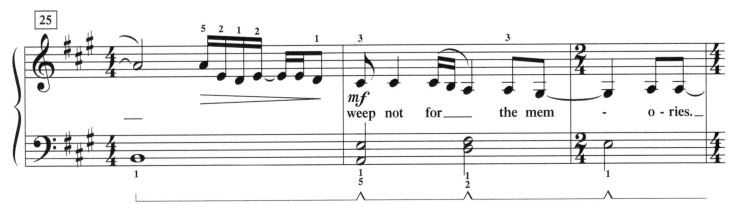

2. So afraid to love you,
   More afraid to lose.
   I'm clinging to a past
   That doesn't let me choose.

Where once there was a darkness,
A deep and endless night,
You gave me everything you had,
Oh, you gave me life. *To Chorus*

"Don't let chords pass you by"

In the **Key of A Major** the *primary* triads (**I, IV, V**) are **A, D**, and **E major**.

chord letter names:	A			D	E			A
scale degrees:	1	2	3	4	5	6	7	8 (1)
Roman numerals:	I			IV	V			I
	tonic			subdominant	dominant			tonic

- Write **A, D, E,** or **E7** in the boxes *above* each staff.
- Write **I, IV, V,** or **V7** in the blanks *below* each staff. (Note: Some chords are in an inversion.)

I Will Remember You

Words and Music by
Sarah McLachlan, Seamus Egan,
and David Merenda

Change the World

Key Signature of E Major

The 4 sharps for E Major:

F# C# G# D#

D# is the *leading tone.*

Key of _____ Major

Music and Words by
Tommy Sims, Gordon Kennedy,
and Wayne Kirkpatrick

Moderately (not fast)

mp If I can reach the stars,
If I could be king

pull one down for you,
e - ven for a day,

shine it on my heart
I'd take you as my queen;

so you could see the truth,
I'd have it no oth - er way.

FF1

then this love I have___ in - side
And our love___ will___ rule___
(in this)

is ev - 'ry - thing it seems.___
king - dom we have made.___

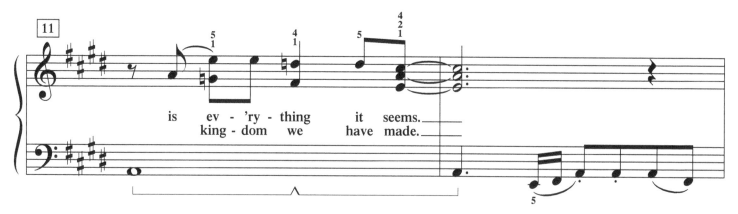

But for now I find___
'Til then I'd be a fool___

'son - ly in my dreams___
wish - ing for the day___
that I can

change_____ the world.___

I will be ___ } the sun - light in your u - ni - verse. ___
would

To Coda ⊕

You would think ___ my love was real - ly some - thing good, ___ if I could ___

change ___ the world.

mf

D.C. al Coda

FF1

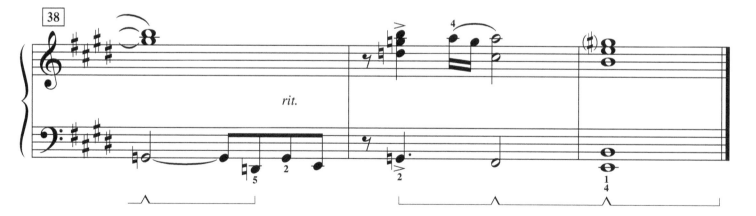

The major scale is made more "bluesy" by flatting *scale degrees 3* and *7*.

DISCOVERY

In the **Key of E Major**, flatting *scale degree 3* (G♯) gives **G natural**; flatting *scale degree 7* (D♯) gives **D natural**.

Find examples of these two "blues notes" in the bass clef and treble clef.

Improvising a Solo

Change the Notes

Improvise means to create "on the spot."

- First, play the "blues scale" shown below, noticing the fingering.

- Then, *listen* as your teacher plays the duet part at the bottom of the page.
  Feel the mood and the beat.

- When you are ready, **improvise** a melody using notes of the blues improvisation scale *in any order*.
  You may wish to begin with the sample melody given. Then continue with your own improvisation.

Optional: Reverse parts. You play the duet part while your teacher or another student improvises.

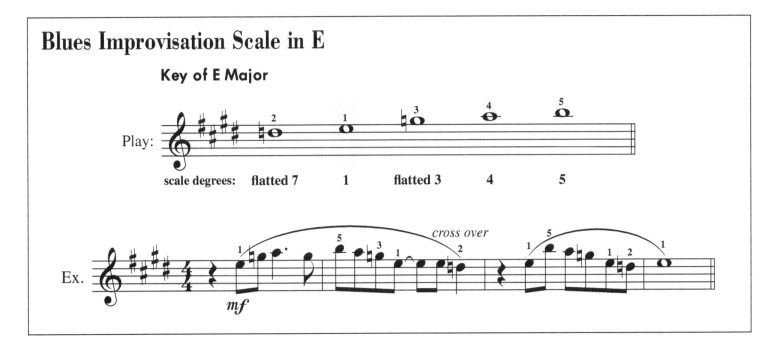

Blues Improvisation Scale in E

Key of E Major

Play:

scale degrees: flatted 7   1   flatted 3   4   5

Ex.

based on music by Tommy Sims,
Gordon Kennedy, and Wayne Kirkpatrick

Teacher Duet: (from *Change the World*)

FF1

Change the Key

Keep the same mood and beat, but **transpose** to the **Key of A**.

- Play the "blues scale" shown below, noticing the fingering.

- *Listen* as your teacher plays the duet part at the bottom of the page.
  Feel the mood and the beat.

- When you are ready, **improvise** a melody using notes of the blues improvisation scale *in any order*.
  You may wish to begin with the sample melody given. Then continue with your own improvisation.

Optional: Reverse parts. You play the duet part while your teacher or another student improvises.

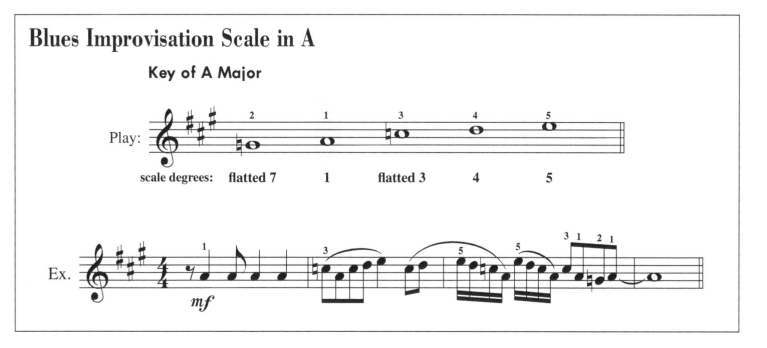

Blues Improvisation Scale in A

Key of A Major

Play:

scale degrees: flatted 7   1   flatted 3   4   5

Ex.

Teacher Duet: (from *Change the World*)

based on music by Tommy Sims,
Gordon Kennedy, and Wayne Kirkpatrick

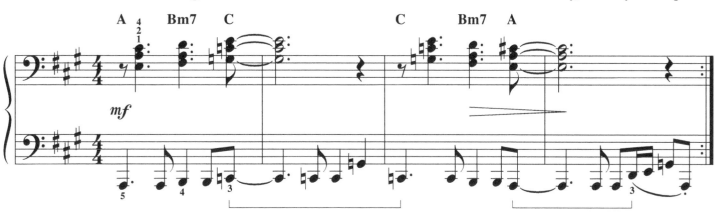

MUSIC DICTIONARY

pp	p	mp	mf	f	ff
pianissimo	*piano*	*mezzo piano*	*mezzo forte*	*forte*	*fortissimo*
very soft	soft	medium soft	medium loud	loud	very loud

crescendo (cresc.)
Play gradually louder.

diminuendo (dim.) or decrescendo (decresc.)
Play gradually softer.

SIGN	TERM	DEFINITION
	accent mark	Play this note louder.
	accidental	A sharp or flat that is not in the key signature. A natural is also an accidental.
	accompaniment	The harmony and rhythm that accompany the melody.
	Alberti bass	A left-hand accompaniment that outlines the notes of a chord using the pattern: *bottom-top-middle-top*.
	arpeggio	The notes of a chord played up or down the keyboard.
	a tempo	Return to the beginning tempo (speed).
	chord	Three or more notes sounding together.
	chord analysis	Naming the chord letter names (Ex. Dm) or the Roman numerals (Ex. I, IV, V7, etc.) of a piece.
	chord symbol	The letter name of the chord indicated above the music. A lower-case "m" is used to show minor.
	chord tone	One of the notes of a chord.
	chorus	A repeated section (music and lyrics) of a song that often features the words of the title.
D.S. al Coda	*Dal Segno al Coda*	Return to the 𝄋 sign and play to the ⊕, then jump to the *Coda*.
	dominant	Step 5 of the scale.
	dominant 7th chord	A four-note chord built in 3rds on the dominant note (scale degree 5) Ex. In the key of C, the dominant 7th chord is G–B–D–F.
	dynamics	The "louds and softs" of music. See dynamic marks above.
	fermata	Hold this note longer than its usual value.
	improvise	To create freely, "on the spot."
	interval	The distance between two musical tones or keys on the keyboard. For example, 2nd, 3rd, 4th, 5th, octave.
	inversion	A rearrangement of the tones of a chord. The 3rd is in the bass for 1st inversion; the 5th is in the bass for 2nd inversion. (See root position.)

FF1